Quicksolve Whodunit Puzzles

Challenging Mini-Mysteries

Jim Sukach

Illustrated by Lucy Corvino

Sterling Publishing Co., Inc. New York

For Jeff and Lynn

Library of Congress Cataloging-in-Publication Data

Sukach, Jim.
    Quicksolve whodunit puzzles : challenging mini-mysteries /
  Jim Sukach ; illustrated by Lucy Corvino.
      p.   cm.
    Includes index.
    Summary: The reader is invited to join celebrated armchair
detective Dr. Jeffrey Lynn Quicksolve in solving a series of mysteries.
The solutions are given in a separate section.
    ISBN 0-8069-0883-1
    1. Literary recreations.   [1. Mystery and detective stories.
    2. Literary recreations.]   I. Corvino, Lucy, ill. II. Title.
PZ7.S9447Qu   1995
[Fic]—dc20
                                          94-47321
                                            CIP
                                            AC

10 9 8

First paperback edition published in 1996 by
Sterling Publishing Company, Inc.
387 Park Avenue South, New York, N.Y. 10016
© 1995 by Jim Sukach
Distributed in Canada by Sterling Publishing
% Canadian Manda Group, One Atlantic Avenue, Suite 105
Toronto, Ontario, Canada M6K 3E7
Distributed in Great Britain and Europe by Cassell PLC
Wellington House, 125 Strand, London WC2R 0BB, England
Distributed in Australia by Capricorn Link (Australia) Pty Ltd.
P.O. Box 6651, Baulkham Hills, Business Centre, NSW 2153, Australia
Manufactured in the United States of America
All rights reserved

Sterling ISBN 0-8069-0883-1 Trade
              0-8069-0884-X Paper

Contents

Dr. J. L. Quicksolve

Dr. Jeffrey Lynn Quicksolve, professor of criminology, retired from the police force as a detective at a very young age. Now he works with various police departments and private detectives as a consultant when he is not teaching at the university.

He certainly knows his business, solving crimes. Many people are amazed at how he solves so many crimes so quickly. When asked how he does it, he replies, "I'm no smarter than anyone else. I just listen very well."

Read, listen, think carefully, and you can solve these crimes too!

Brotherly Love

•••••••••

Tom and Pat Pennysworth were two extremely wealthy brothers. Tom had been missing for two days. Dr. J. L. Quicksolve was at their house talking to Pat.

"When did you last see your brother?" Dr. Quicksolve asked.

"Saturday afternoon, around two o'clock, a tall, blond woman came here to pick him up. I guess they had a date. They drove away in her car, and I haven't seen Tom since then," Pat explained. Just then the phone rang, and Pat answered it. "It's for you," he said, handing the phone to Quicksolve.

"J. L. Quicksolve," he said into the phone.

"Dr. Quicksolve," came the response, "this is Officer Dennis. We've found the body of Tom Pennysworth out here at his cottage on Silver Lake. He's been shot to death."

"Any clues, Officer Dennis?" Quicksolve asked.

"No, We're still looking."

"Let me know right away if you find anything. Good-bye."

"What is it?" Pat Pennysworth asked as the detective hung up the phone and turned to him.

"I'm afraid it's bad news. Your brother's been found. He's dead," said Dr. Quicksolve.

"Oh, no!" Pat cried.

"Where were you on Saturday evening, Pat?"

"I was right here! You can't suspect me! I didn't go anywhere near the cottage!" Pat shouted.

"I think you did, Pat," Dr. Quicksolve stated coolly.

Why does he suspect the brother?

Solution on page 90.

Station Stickup

Dr. J. L. Quicksolve and his son, J. L. Jr., pulled into the gas station, and Dr. Quicksolve got out of the car. He said, "Fill up the gas tank, Junior, while I get this robbery report."

"But the sign says 'Prepay,' Dad. Oh, I see, it says, 'Prepay after 5:00 p.m.' OK," Junior said as he got out and went to pump the gas.

The station attendant was explaining what had happened when Junior came in. "Two men pulled up to the pump there, right where you're parked, and pumped their gas. They filled their tank, and one came in as if to pay. Then he drew a gun from inside his jacket and said, 'This is a stickup!' I gave him the money, about two hundred dollars. He ran back to the car, and they drove off."

"Can you describe the two men?" asked Dr. Quicksolve.

"Sure, they were both tall, about six feet or a little more. The one that came in had a moustache and a scar on his left cheek," explained the attendant.

"There was no one else around?" Quicksolve asked.

"No, it was around 10:30, and we don't do a lot of business after 10:00 at night," the attendant said. "I was all alone here."

"Wait a minute, Dad. Something sounds fishy here!" Junior exclaimed.

"I think I know what you mean, Junior. Maybe the attendant can explain it to us," Dr. Quicksolve said, turning to the attendant.

What had Junior figured out?

Solution on page 90.

Backyard Bandit

•••••••••

Dr. J. L. Quicksolve arrived at the home of Mr. and Mrs. John Mark. Mrs. Mark came to the door and let him in. She and Mr. Mark explained that they had been robbed while they were away for the weekend. They said their neighbor had seen the burglar. Dr. Quicksolve asked to talk with the neighbor, Mr. Dare.

John Mark led Dr. Quicksolve out the back door. Mr. Dare was on a ladder on the other side of an eight-foot hedge that separated the two backyards. John introduced Dr. Quicksolve and Mr. Dare. "Dr. Quicksolve would like to ask you a few questions," John said.

"I told the police officer everything, but, sure, I don't mind," Mr. Dare said.

"Just tell me what you saw, Mr. Dare," Quicksolve said.

"Well, it happened this morning. I was mowing the grass here in my backyard. I heard a funny noise over here, and I saw a man at John's back door, picking the lock. He got inside pretty quickly. I ran into my house and called the police. Just before they got here I saw him run out the back door carrying a large box. The police were just a few minutes too late."

"Could you describe the man?" Dr. Quicksolve asked.

"Sure. The police have the description," Mr. Dare said.

"I guess it doesn't really matter, unless you described yourself," Dr. Quicksolve said.

Why does Dr. Quicksolve suspect Mr. Dare?

Solution on page 90.

The Doubtable Burglary

David Doubtable was showing Dr. J. L. Quicksolve the window that had obviously been jimmied open by the burglar. The glass had not been broken, but the window had been forced open with some sort of pry bar. "Let's go outside and see if we can find out anything there," Dr. Quicksolve suggested.

Mr. Doubtable led him out the back door and right to the window that had been pried open. Searching the bushes beneath the window, the detective found a large screwdriver, apparently the tool used to pry the window open. "Oh, that's mine," said Mr. Doubtable, taking the screwdriver. "I'll put it away downstairs."

Mr. Doubtable then took Dr. Quicksolve through the house, showing him what had been stolen. "Adding up the value of my wife's missing jewelry, the television, stereo, and everything, the value comes to over fifty-thousand dollars. It's a good thing I'm insured."

"Was anything taken from the basement, Mr. Doubtable?" Quicksolve asked.

"No, I was lucky there. I have a lot of valuable tools down there, but there's no evidence the burglar even went downstairs. It looks like he knew what he wanted and went mainly for the expensive jewelry," was his reply.

"It looks like he, or should I say you, chose the expensive and highly insured items. Am I right, Mr. Doubtable?"

Why did Dr. Quicksolve suspect Mr. Doubtable was lying?

Solution on page 90.

Locker Caper

•••••••

Dr. J. L. Quicksolve was visiting his son's junior high school. He was talking to the assistant principal, Mr. Paddlebottom, when there was a knock at the door of the office. A young seventh-grade boy stepped into the room. "I'm sorry to bother you, Mr. Paddlebottom, but I have an emergency!"

"What kind of an emergency, Bennie?" Mr. Paddlebottom asked.

"I brought some videotapes to lend to a friend. I had them in my book bag, and I put that in my locker as soon as I got to school. When I went back to my locker after lunch they were gone!"

"Bennie, you know you're not supposed to bring videotapes to school," Mr. Paddlebottom said.

"But I never even took them out of the bag! I was going to lend them to Skeeter after school."

"Maybe I can help," Dr. Quicksolve interrupted. "Bennie, do you have any idea who might have taken them?"

"Well, Jason has the locker next to mine, and I think he's watched me open my locker enough to learn my combination. Besides that, the teacher let him leave the room this morning to go to the rest room."

Mr. Paddlebottom sent Bennie to his class, and he asked the secretary to get Jason. When Jason came in, Mr. Paddlebottom introduced him to Dr. Quicksolve, but he didn't mention he was a detective.

"We just wondered, Jason, if you have heard anything about Bennie's locker being broken into, since yours is right next to his," Dr. Quicksolve said.

"No, I don't know anything, and I didn't see anybody. I don't know who would want those tapes, anyway," he stated.

"I think Mr. Paddlebottom might go a little easier on you if you would tell us the truth right now, Jason," Dr. Quicksolve said.

Why was Dr. Quicksolve so sure about Jason?

Solution on page 90.

Cross-Eyed Witness
•••••••••

Dr. J. L. Quicksolve noticed he was in one of those older neighborhoods where the houses were all almost exactly alike, lined up evenly side-by-side, and very close together. Finally he found the right number, the Wilsons.

The Wilsons were still away on vacation. The only ones there to meet the detective were the uniformed policeman, Officer Dennis, and the next-door neighbor, Mr. Menace, who had called the police and reported the burglary. Dr. Quicksolve introduced himself and asked Mr. Menace to explain what he had seen.

"I had just turned out the lights to go to bed when I heard a crash. I looked out my bedroom window just in time to see two men break down the Wilsons' door and go inside. I stayed right there at that front window and saw them carry some things out to their van and drive away. Then I called the police right away," Mr. Menace explained.

"Did you get a good look at the men or the van?" Dr. Quicksolve asked.

"I got a pretty good look at them. My bedroom window faces right out to the front street, but I couldn't see their faces or get a license-plate number. I guess I'm not much help."

Dr. Quicksolve examined the scene. He noticed the back door had been broken right off its hinges. The inside of the house was messed up quite a bit, but he had no idea what was stolen yet. A street light provided a good view of the street. Walking out into the street, he looked up at the next house, and then he could see the light was still on in Mr. Menace's bedroom.

He came back to the house and said, "Mr. Menace, the Wilsons aren't here to tell us what's missing, but I'm sure you know exactly, don't you?"

Why did he suspect Mr. Menace?

Solution on page 90.

Flying Thief

●●●●●●●●●

Dr. J. L. Quicksolve was flying out to Colorado to visit his aunt and uncle. He had been talking to the lady beside him, Miss Pettithief, for quite some time. When she learned that he was a detective she was eager to share her story with him.

"I was so upset after the robbery that I had to take time off and take a vacation," she explained.

"Tell me about the robbery," Dr. Quicksolve said.

"I was the only teller on duty at my bank at the time. The thing is, the robbery happened just at the time we had a power failure. A man walked up to my window and handed me a note that said to hand over the money, and that he had a gun. I stepped on the silent alarm, but apparently nothing happened because the electricity had gone out. So the man got away," she told the detective.

"Did they catch the robber?" Quicksolve asked.

"No, he got away. They did get a picture of him on the bank's security camera, but the camera just showed my back and the top of his head. It didn't even show me handing over the money, but I could see enough in the video to tell it was the robber."

"Was the robber someone you had seen before?" Dr. Quicksolve asked.

"No, I had never seen him before, but I did give a description," Miss Pettithief said.

"I bet the thief is about your height, your weight, with your hair and eye color. Am I right?" Quicksolve asked.

Why does he suspect her?

Solution on page 90.

Reflection of a Crime

••••••••

Dr. Quicksolve was at the police station, and Sergeant Stratefellow asked for help with a mugging case. Miss Dimlite had been robbed right on the street while shopping.

"We had a suspect, but we had to let him go. We were sure he was the one. He fit the description almost perfectly. He even had a scar on his face like the one the victim described, but that turned out to be a problem. You see, the scar was on the wrong side of his face. Here's the drawing our artist made. It's just like she described him." The sergeant handed Dr. Quicksolve the drawing of a man with a moustache and a large scar on his left cheek.

"Let me talk to Miss Dimlite," Dr. Quicksolve said. Sergeant Stratefellow took him into the next room and introduced him to Miss Dimlite.

Showing her the drawing, he asked, "Miss Dim-lite, you're sure this drawing is accurate? It looks just like the man who robbed you, in every detail?"

"Oh, yes. I'll never forget that face. He grabbed me from behind and pushed me up against the store window. He held my arm behind me so I couldn't move. He took my purse and ran off. It happened so fast, I don't think I took a breath through the whole thing!" Miss Dimlite explained, remembering the crime.

"If he came from behind, how did you see his face so well?" Dr. Quicksolve asked.

"Why, I saw his reflection in the window, of course!" she replied.

"Sergeant, get your suspect back here!" Dr. Quicksolve exclaimed.

Why did he say that?

Solution on page 90.

A Puzzling Story

Mrs. Charmsworth and her son Leroy were telling Dr. J. L. Quicksolve about the burglary.

"Leroy and I had gone to a concert when the burglary occurred," she explained.

"Was anyone here when you left?" he asked.

"No, Mary, the maid, had left shortly after dinner. Leroy was ready early, and he was working on his puzzle on the kitchen table. He'd finished all but one piece that he couldn't find. We had to hurry out the door."

"What did you find when you came home?" the detective asked.

"Right away we noticed the door was open, and when we came in we noticed a lot of things missing—the stereo, the TV, the computer. I don't know what else, yet," Mrs. Charmsworth explained.

"What can you tell me, Leroy?"

"Well, I know the door was locked. I was in a hurry, but I'm sure I locked it," Leroy explained.

Later Dr. Quicksolve questioned Mary, the maid. "When did you leave the house, Mary?" he asked her.

"I left right after I cleaned up after supper. I did the dishes and swept the kitchen. I remember I found that last piece to Leroy's puzzle, and I put it on the puzzle, checked the dining area to be sure I had gotten everything, and then I left," Mary explained.

"So you left before Mrs. Charmsworth and Leroy left for the concert?"

"Yes, I'm sure of that. They had gone upstairs to begin getting ready," Mary replied.

"I'm sure you had some help to carry all of those things, Mary. Why don't you tell me all about the burglars you brought in here?"

Why does Dr. Quicksolve suspect Mary?

Solution on page 91.

Inside Job

••••••••

Dr. J. L. Quicksolve drove slowly down the dark country road, shining his spotlight on the mailboxes. When he found the one that said, "Ted Victom," he turned. He drove up the long driveway to the large house. A butler answered the door and showed him in.

Ted Victom explained that he had been robbed during the night. "Did you see or hear anything suspicious?" asked Dr. Quicksolve.

"No, I'm a sound sleeper, and I wear earplugs besides. I just discovered my safe open and my money gone when James, my butler, woke me up about an hour ago," Mr. Victom explained.

"What about your wife? Did she see anything?"

"No, she was asleep too. She's upstairs right now. She'll be down to talk to you in a minute," Mr. Victom replied.

"Let me talk to your butler then," said Dr. Quicksolve. Mr. Victom called in his butler, and the detective asked him to describe what he had seen.

James said, "I was asleep in my quarters when I was awakened by a slamming door. I got up and looked out the front window just in time to see a man get into a red car out on the road."

"Can you describe the man?" asked the detective.

"He had red hair, a thin red mustache, and a small scar above his right eye. He wore black pants and a black shirt," James answered, describing the suspect.

"I won't have to talk to your wife after all, Mr. Victom. We have the robber right here," Dr. Quicksolve stated firmly.

What does he mean?

Solution on page 91.

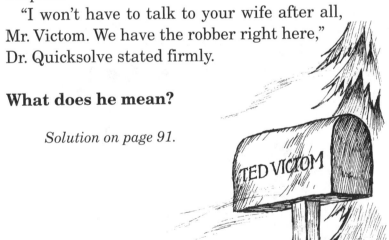

Welcome Bandit

•••••••••

Dr. J. L. Quicksolve stood at the large oak door and rang the bell. He watched through the large, beautifully etched glass window in the door as Mr. Gulibull came and let him in. "I understand you've been robbed," he said to Mr. Gulibull. "I'm J. L. Quicksolve. You called."

"Yes, Dr. Quicksolve, thank you for getting here so soon."

"Tell me what happened, Mr. Gulibull."

"Well, Germain, our butler, went to answer the door when the bell rang. As soon as he opened this door, the man who was standing here rushed in and

knocked him down. Then the stranger pulled a gun and made Germain show him where my wife's jewelry is kept. He got away with a lot of jewelry and several other valuable items. He hit Germain over the head before he finally left."

"Is Germain here now?" asked Quicksolve.

"Yes, he's upstairs lying down," answered Mr. Gulibull.

"Did he tell you what the robber looked like?" asked Quicksolve.

"No, he says the bandit wore a mask, so he wasn't able to see his face at all," Mr. Gulibull explained.

"Do you think Germain is well enough to be arrested?" asked Dr. Quicksolve.

Why arrest Germain?

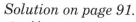

Solution on page 91.

Holey Donuts

Dr. J. L. Quicksolve arrived at the scene of the robbery, the office of the Dee Dee Donuts Company. Gerald Cremefil was being questioned by a uniformed policeman, Officer Longshot. Mr. Cremefil was just explaining what happened. "I was sitting here at my desk. I heard someone come in. Before I could turn around someone hit me on the head. He tied me to my chair and blindfolded me. He had a gun and he forced me to open the safe. He took all the money and then he left."

"Can you describe the robber, Mr. Cremefil?" Dr. Quicksolve asked.

"No, like I said, I was blindfolded," Mr. Cremefil responded.

"What did you do after the robber left?" Quicksolve asked then.

"Well, after he left I rocked my chair back and forth until I fell over. The chair broke, and I was able to

untie myself. It probably took me half an hour or so to get loose. When I did, of course, I called the police right away," Mr. Cremefil explained.

"Mr. Cremefil," said Dr. Quicksolve, "I'm afraid there's a hole in your story bigger than the holes in your donuts. Now tell us the truth about this."

Why did Dr. Quicksolve suspect Mr. Cremefil?

Solution on page 91.

Breakfast Break-In

· · · · · · · ·

Dr. J. L. Quicksolve was sitting at his breakfast table when he got the call about the burglary.

Mrs. Mula met him at the door and asked him in. He had just introduced himself when he heard a shrill whistle from the back of the house. It was the tea kettle. Mrs. Mula excused herself to tend to it.

"Come in the kitchen and sit down," she said. "We can have some tea. The maid hasn't come in yet," she explained.

"Tell me about your robbery, Mrs. Mula," the detective said.

"Well, someone must have come in before I got up, I guess," she told him. "I got up this morning, and I came down here and put water on for tea. Then I went back upstairs. That's when I heard someone down here. I shouted down that I have a gun and that I was calling the police. I heard him run out the back door, but I didn't see anything. When I came downstairs I saw the safe was open and my jewelry was gone. I turned and came right back upstairs to my room and called you. I was afraid to come back downstairs until I heard you at the door just now."

"I was up when you called, but it still took me at least twenty minutes to get here. I think there's a problem with your story, Mrs. Mula. Is your jewelry insured?"

"Oh, yes, of course," Mrs. Mula responded.

"Somehow I knew you'd say that. You must be having some problems, Mrs. Mula, to try to get insurance money like this. Tell me about it," said Dr. Quicksolve.

Why does Dr. Quicksolve suspect Mrs. Mula?

Solution on page 91.

Rose's Robbery

••••••••

Dr. J. L. Quicksolve was greeted at the door of Cindy's Flower Shop by Cindy herself. "It looks like we've been robbed, Dr. Quicksolve," she said.

"Tell me what happened," the detective said.

"My assistant, Rose Thornbush, was taking our cash to the bank when she was robbed. I'll let her give you the details." Turning to a short, dark-haired woman who had just entered the room, she said, "Rose, this is Dr. J. L. Quicksolve. Tell him what happened."

"I'm still pretty upset," she said, "and there isn't a lot to tell."

"Just start from the beginning and tell me all you can remember," Quicksolve told her.

"I was on my way to the bank with the bag of money. I had just taken my keys out of my purse to unlock my car when a man came up behind me and stuck a gun in my back. He said, 'Give me the money and your keys, or I'll shoot.' He took the money, locked me in the car, and then he ran off. By the time I was able to get out of the car he was long gone. I guess we'll never see him or that money again."

Dr. Quicksolve grinned and said, "No, we won't see him, but we will see the money as soon as you tell us where you put it. I can't believe you thought we would accept that story. Is this a joke?"

What is so wrong with her story?

Solution on page 91.

Skating Rink Robbery

....

Dr. Quicksolve entered the skating rink building. You could hear the loud music they played, even in the lobby. In the main room where the skaters skated around and around, you could hardly carry on a conversation because of the loud music.

The manager, Mr. Blade, came over to the detective and signalled for him to come through a nearby door marked "Office." When they went in and closed the door you couldn't hear the music, and they could talk.

Two men were sitting in the office. One was holding an ice pack to his head.

"I had this room made soundproof to keep out the loud music the teenagers like so much. The problem is, we've been robbed. I just got here myself, so I'll let my employees, Frank and Joe, tell you what happened. Joe, you go first."

The one with the ice pack spoke up. "I was in here counting the money. I was sitting here with my back to the door and someone came in behind me and hit me over the head. When I came to, the money was gone."

"What can you tell us?" Dr. Quicksolve asked, turning towards Frank.

"I was out in the main room watching the skaters. I heard a crash from the office here, and I turned around just in time to see a tall man slip out of the office and run out of the building. I came in and found Joe unconscious. I woke him and called the police."

"So where did you hide the money so quickly, Frank?" Dr. Quicksolve asked.

Why did Dr. Quicksolve suspect Frank?

Solution on page 91.

Ransom Rescue

● ● ● ● ● ● ● ● ●

Dolores Dollars had been kidnapped. A ransom note had been sent to her father demanding that two hundred thousand dollars be brought to an abandoned cabin in a remote forest area. The money was delivered, and the police had cautiously closed in from all sides. Dolores was found in the cabin blindfolded and tied up, but unharmed. She said she had been attacked from behind and kept blindfolded. She had not seen her attacker.

The police had picked up two men immediately who had been found in the area. They were sure that one was the kidnapper. They called in Dr. J. L. Quicksolve to help.

"So you have two suspects, John Dill and Frank Sweet," said Dr. Quicksolve.

"That's right," said Officer Kautchya.

"What are their alibis?"

"John claims he was out hunting and never saw the girl or anyone else. He says he's innocent, and he wants to be put in a lineup right away so he can prove it and go home. Frank says that he was just hiking in the mountains. He says he saw a few cars, but he didn't pay much attention to them. He claims he didn't kidnap the girl, and he's anxious to take a lie-detector test to prove it," said the officer.

"Get Frank's address and let him go home, but I think you'd better keep John," said Dr. Quicksolve.

Why John?

Solution on page 91.

Barefoot Liar

• • • • • • • •

Mr. Crookby answered the door in his pajamas and bare feet. He let Dr. Quicksolve into the house. They introduced themselves to each other, and then Crookby began telling the detective about the robbery.

"The burglar must have come in through this window. You can see it was broken from the outside because the glass is spread halfway across the room," he explained.

It was apparent that the window had been broken from the outside. Glass was spread past the fallen telephone stand, and the phone lay on the floor in the middle of the glass. It was upright with the receiver in its place.

"And where were you when the window was broken, Mr. Crookby?"

"I was in bed. The crash must have woken me up, but I'm afraid I didn't react very quickly because I didn't realize what it was. I thought it was a cat or dog outside in the garbage cans or something. When I got up this morning and saw this mess, I called the police right away," he said.

"Did you use this phone here?" asked Dr. Quicksolve.

"Yes, I did. It was the closest one," Crookby said.

"Well, that explains why the receiver is in its place after being knocked to the floor, but there is one thing I think you can't explain," said Dr. Quicksolve.

What is it?

Solution on page 92.

Pennyroll's Money Bags

•••••••••

Dr. J. L. Quicksolve had come to Mr. Pennyroll's house. Mr. Pennyroll was explaining how he had been kidnapped by bank robbers when he arrived to open up the bank where he was assistant manager.

"They forced me to open up the safe and give them the money. Then they made me drive towards home from the bank. They intended to get my wife's jewels," explained Mr. Pennyroll.

"Tell me how you were able to escape, Mr. Pennyroll," said Dr. Quicksolve.

"We were driving towards my house from the bank. One of the kidnappers had dumped the money out of the bank bag into a paper sack. Then he threw the bank bag out of the window. Two blocks later we stopped for a red light. He was looking down at the money, and I saw my chance. I opened my door, jumped out of the car, and ran. I ran up to the nearest house, and they let me in. Luckily, the kidnappers didn't follow. They just drove off."

"Let's follow your route back to the bank and see if we can find any clues," said the detective.

They left the house in Dr. Quicksolve's car. Soon Pennyroll shouted, "There it is! The money bag!" They stopped and picked up the empty bank bag and continued on towards the bank. In a few minutes they came to a light. "This is where I escaped," said Pennyroll.

"I have a problem with your story," said Dr. Quicksolve.

What's the problem?

Solution on page 92.

Jacked Up

Dr. J. L. Quicksolve was awakened by the sounds of his dog barking downstairs in the front hall by the door. He jumped out of bed and looked out his window to see his car jacked up on one side, and two young men trying to remove his wheel. Quicksolve opened the window and shouted at the two men. They ran to their car, backed out, and sped away as Quicksolve dashed to the phone and called the police station. They had a car in the area and called it immediately.

Quicksolve slipped on his pants and ran downstairs and outside. He had just finished examining his car when the police car turned into the drive. There were two officers in the front seat and two other men in the back seat. When the police car came to a halt, the driver got out and walked over to Dr. Quicksolve.

"We caught these two speeding away from the area as soon as we got the call. We searched the car, but we didn't find any evidence we can use," said the officer.

"Did you search the trunk of the car?" asked Dr. Quicksolve.

"Yes, we did. Except for their own spare tire, it was absolutely empty. I don't think we really have anything to hold them on right now."

"Well, I think you do. It's not what you found, but what you didn't find. Arrest them and check for prints later," said Quicksolve.

What evidence was he talking about?

Solution on page 92.

Now You See It

• • • • • • • • •

Frank Lee was telling Dr. J. L. Quicksolve about the robbery. "I always take a ride into the mountains on my motorcycle for about an hour. I leave right at four o'clock. Just before I left I had been writing letters in the den, where the missing paintings had been hanging. They were there then, so I know they were taken while I was gone. This time I was about an hour late getting back because I ran out of gas, and I had to push the motorcycle home."

"Didn't you check the gas tank?" asked Dr. Quicksolve.

"Well, no, because I always fill it up when I get back. I thought I filled it last night. But I could have forgotten," answered Mr. Lee.

"Was anyone here in the house while you were gone?" asked Quicksolve.

"Yes, the cook was here, but he was in the kitchen at the back of the house. It's not very close to the den, and he says he didn't hear anything."

"So you noticed the paintings were missing right away when you got back?" asked the detective.

"Not really. The cook was just setting the table, as he always is just as I get back from my ride, so I ate right away, as usual. After dinner I went into my den to read and have a little coffee. That's when I noticed the paintings were gone," explained Mr. Lee.

"I'm afraid your cook has cooked up more than dinner, Mr. Lee," announced Dr. Quicksolve.

Why does Dr. Quicksolve suspect the cook?

Solution on page 92.

McMugger

·········

The young teenager described the boy who had knocked him down and taken his wallet. He also gave a description of the car his assailant had driven away in, a black convertible.

Tom Tait was stopped while driving near the area. He fit the description, and so did his car. The young teenager identified Tom as the one who robbed him. Tom denied it.

Dr. Quicksolve questioned him about where he was during the robbery.

"I was sitting in a hamburger place eating at that time. I must have been there for twenty minutes," Tait said.

"So if you were there that long somebody who works there should be able to back up your story, right?" said Dr. Quicksolve.

"Well, no. I took my tray and sat in the back. I don't think anybody saw me for more than a minute, even though I sat there a long time and finished eating there," Tait said.

"It seems to be your word against the word of the young victim here. It looks bad for you, unless you can give some reason why this boy might lie, or else come up with a better alibi yourself," said Dr. Quicksolve.

"Wait a minute! There's something in my car, the bag from the hamburger place. That's proof I was there!" exclaimed Tait.

"I think you've had it, Tom. You can bag that story of yours," said the detective.

What gave Tom away?

Solution on page 92.

Fred Fraudstop

· · · · · · · · ·

Fred Fraudstop called Dr. J. L. Quicksolve, the famous detective, with an offer from the insurance company he worked for as an insurance investigator in Beverly Hills. Mr. Fraudstop's job was to investigate insurance claims. He tried to make sure they were legitimate claims and to find out if things were really stolen or lost. If they were, his job was to try to find them. Lately he felt he had been getting a lot of claims that were not legitimate. People were claiming expensive things were stolen, for example, when they really were not. The person making the claim would sell or keep the item and get money from the insurance company too!

Fred thought Dr. Quicksolve could help, so he invited him to come and stay in Beverly Hills for several weeks and look into a few cases with him. Dr. Quicksolve accepted the offer, and he was on his way to Beverly Hills.

Dark Shadows

●●●●●●●●

The first claim Mr. Fraudstop wanted help with involved Mr. Richard Grimsox. Mr. Grimsox claimed a burglar had broken into his house and stolen his wife's $15,000 necklace.

Dr. Quicksolve was in Mr. Fraudstop's office discussing a case when Richard Grimsox called to make his insurance claim. Fraudstop told Mr. Grimsox he would be right over.

It was one of those rainy afternoons made for a mystery. But now the drizzle of rain that had been ceaseless for days finally came to a stop, and the sky began to clear. Mr. Fraudstop and Dr. Quicksolve walked up the steps of the old mansion and rang the doorbell. Richard Grimsox opened the door himself. "Hello, Mr. Fraudstop," he said, looking uncomfortably at Dr. Quicksolve.

"This is Dr. Jeffrey Lynn Quicksolve, Mr. Grimsox," Fraudstop explained. "He has agreed to help us out."

"Yes, I recognize you from pictures I've seen in the paper, Dr. Quicksolve," Mr. Grimsox said as he reached out to shake the detective's hand.

"Hello, Mr. Grimsox," Dr. Quicksolve said. "You've had a burglary?"

"Yes, it happened while I was upstairs sleeping, about three o'clock this morning. I heard noises and looked out the window. I didn't see anyone. They must have been too close to the house. I only saw shadows of two men. I heard a car start up and drive away. I turned the lights on and ran downstairs. I found my wall safe wide open," Mr. Grimsox explained.

"Was there a lot of money in the safe?" Dr. Quicksolve asked.

"No, only about three hundred dollars, but my wife's fifteen-thousand-dollar necklace was also gone, as I told Mr. Fraudstop over the phone. I just thank God that that necklace was insured. That would be quite a loss to take."

"And Mrs. Grimsox was with you all of the time?" the detective continued.

"Yes, she was, but she didn't get up until after I called the police," Grimsox answered.

"I guess the only real question now is, was your wife in on this attempt of yours to get the insurance company to pay off on something that hasn't been stolen?" Dr. Quicksolve stated.

"What are you talking about? You can't prove a thing like that!" Mr. Grimsox cried.

"I think I can, beyond the shadow of a doubt," Dr. Quicksolve replied.

Why did Dr. Quicksolve suspect Mr. Grimsox?

Solution on page 92.

Crooked Interview

●●●●●●●●●

Dr. Quicksolve told Fred Fraudstop he had called an old friend who lived in California. His name was Bob Bullion, and he managed the Safe-N-Sure Security Company. Mr. Bullion had invited Dr. Quicksolve to stop by and see his company. Dr. Quicksolve knew that Fred, being an insurance investigator, would be very interested in learning a little more about a local security company, so he asked him to go along with him.

Fred was happy to have the invitation, so they met for lunch and drove out to the Safe-N-Sure Security Company early that afternoon.

Bob Bullion took Dr. Quicksolve and Fred Fraudstop into a small room with a one-way mirror that let them see into the next room without being seen.

"I have people interviewing potential employees in the next room. We check their backgrounds for criminal records, of course, but we also have extensive interviews to give us an idea about the person before we give out a gun. Let's listen for a minute or two."

The man applying for the job and being interviewed in the next room had a name tag that said "Carl Crook." Fred Fraudstop laughed and said, "It's funny, but that name 'Crook' rings a bell. Have you checked his record?"

"No, not yet. Wait, I think our interviewer is about to ask him about that," Bob said. They paused and listened as the interviewer asked Carl if he had ever been in prison.

"No, I've never been near a prison. Those screws scare me, and I can't stand bars. That's why I want to work in an armored car. You get to move around and not just stay in one place," Carl Crook answered.

"You'd better check this one's record pretty well, Bob. You might give an ex-convict a chance to work for you, but I think this guy is lying," Dr. Quicksolve told his friend.

Why does he suspect Carl Crook?

Solution on page 92.

Cool Mickey
••••••••

Dr. J. L. Quicksolve was packing his things on his last day in Beverly Hills. He was anxious to return to his family.

"A young woman, Betty Finn, who had a life insurance policy from us, has died," Fred Fraudstop explained to Dr. Quicksolve. "It looks like she may have been murdered by her best friend right in her own apartment."

"Did she have a fight with this friend?" Dr. Quicksolve asked.

"The police say they can't find any evidence of a fight or any motive. That's what puzzles them," Fred responded.

"Whose name was on the policy as beneficiary?"

"Her husband, of course, but he was out of the apartment when it happened."

Quicksolve asked, "How was she killed?"

"Poison," was the response.

"Let's go talk to this friend," Dr. Quicksolve said, getting up from his chair.

They arrived at the home of Mary Scapegoat, the accused friend. She was home on bail, and she came to the door.

Mr. Fraudstop introduced himself and Dr. Quicksolve. Then he asked if they could ask her a few questions. She was obviously upset about what had happened, but she said yes, she would be glad to answer questions. She let them in and began talking.

"I don't know how she was poisoned. I just know that I didn't do it," Mary Scapegoat told them.

"Tell me just what happened," Dr. Quicksolve said.

"Betty, her husband Mickey, and I were at their house. Mickey went to the kitchen to make drinks for us. When he brought the drinks out, he took a little sip of Betty's drink just before he gave it to

her. She complained and said he gave her too much ice to begin with and then he had the nerve to drink some of hers. He laughed and said he was going to get some beer. Then he left. He'd been gone about ten or fifteen minutes when Betty collapsed and fell to the floor. I couldn't wake her, so I called an ambulance. Mickey got home just as the ambulance pulled away. I think he poisoned her, but I can't prove it, especially since I said I saw him drink from her glass. I was the last one with her, so I was arrested. I didn't do it, and I'm willing to take a lie detector test!"

"I think you'll probably pass that lie detector test, too, but I'm not so sure about Mickey. I can think of one way he might have done it," said Dr. Quicksolve.

How?

Solution on page 93.

Missing Money

• • • • • • • •

Dr. J. L. Quicksolve was glad to be home. He and his son, Junior, walked out of their yard and turned up their sidewalk. Junior had their dog, Copper, a golden retriever, on a leash. They were going for a walk.

It was a beautiful day for a walk. It was warm and sunny. There were people working in their yards or riding by on bikes. Two young men were walking on either side of the street, going from house to house, probably selling magazines. Quicksolve nodded his head and said hello as he passed one of the two salesmen going in the opposite direction.

A neighbor, Mr. Shortabreath, and his wife passed by, jogging together. They stopped and walked back to talk to Dr. Quicksolve and Junior and to pet Copper.

Mr. Shortabreath said hello and then, "I tried to call you last night, Jeff. You know I'm chairman of our Neighborhood Lookout Committee. Well, several people over on our street have reported things missing lately."

"What kind of things?" Dr. Quicksolve asked.

"Strange things, like money right out of their purses, or small valuable items, like jewelry. It's always something small. There's never any sign of a break-in, and so little is missing that they don't notice it right away. They even find it hard to say when the things were taken. They usually suspect their kids or their kids' friends. It's pretty strange."

Turning to Junior, Quicksolve said, "Junior, run home through the backyards and unlock the front door. Then wait in the backyard. I'll take Copper and be there in a minute."

What is Dr. Quicksolve doing?

Solution on page 93.

Motorcycle Mischief

● ● ● ● ● ● ● ● ●

Dr. J. L. Quicksolve came into the police station to invite his friend Sergeant Rebekah Shurshot to lunch. When he walked into her office, he saw a young man and a young woman sitting in chairs and talking with Sergeant Shurshot. The man was speaking. He had crutches leaning against his chair, and his right knee was bandaged.

"I didn't steal her motorcycle," he was saying. "You can see someone hit me with their car door when I pulled up to a stoplight. He swung his door open and hit my leg right here." He pointed to the bandage. "I only had the one leg on the ground because I had just stopped, and my other foot was on the brake. So I fell over when that door hit me. I was trying to get up when another guy jumped out of the car, pushed me down, and took off on the motorcycle. It all happened so fast that I couldn't do anything about it!"

Sergeant Shurshot smiled at Dr. Quicksolve and asked him to sit down. "Marcie," she said to Dr. Quicksolve, indicating the young lady, "was trying to sell her motorcycle. Tom, here, took it for a test ride. But then he called Marcie and told her it had been stolen. Marcie thinks he stole it. I'm trying to get the story about what happened."

"Tom, have you ridden motorcycles much?" Dr. Quicksolve asked the young man.

"Quite a bit, but I've never owned one before. I just finished the Rider's Safety Course, and I got a license. I liked her bike. I probably would have bought it, but I didn't steal it," Tom said.

"I think you did, Tom," Dr. Quicksolve said.

Why doesn't he believe Tom's story?

Solution on page 93.

Bop-n-Rob
•••••••••

Dr. J. L. Quicksolve walked into the furniture store and was directed to an office area in the back of the store where his friend Sergeant Rebekah Shurshot was talking to the manager. The manager was holding a towel to the back of his head above his left ear. Two men were sitting at a small table behind them. Each of them was writing frantically on a sheet of paper. They looked like a mirror image of each other with their heads down over the papers they were concentrating on so intently. Dr. Quicksolve discovered why they were writing when Sergeant Shurshot explained.

"Dr. Quicksolve, thanks for coming right over. Mr. Drumhead, here, is the manager of the store. He said

he was facing the front of the store with his back to this office area when he was hit from behind and robbed. He thought he was alone in the store, and he's sure no one could have sneaked by him into the office. That means one of these two men here, assistant managers, are the only ones who could have been back there. They both have keys and could have come in the back door. I asked them to write out their explanations of where they were and what they were doing at the time of the robbery. You can question them now, Dr. Quicksolve."

"I don't think that will be necessary, Sergeant Shurshot. It looks like you have already solved the crime, and we can tell who probably did it right now," Dr. Quicksolve said.

How could Dr. Quicksolve solve this one so quickly?

Solution on page 93.

Boat Bash

•••••••••

Dr. J. L. Quicksolve was glad to be out of the hot sun and in the air-conditioned offices of the police station listening to Officer Kautchya, who was talking about the couple he was about to question. "There was a boating accident. A small speedboat ran into a rowboat with two young girls aboard, but fortunately, they were thrown out of the boat and aren't hurt, just shaken. The guy in the speedboat has a record of reckless and drunk driving in his boat already. He's sure to go to jail if he's convicted this time," Officer Kautchya explained. Then he invited Dr. Quicksolve to help with the questioning.

Officer Kautchya introduced himself and Dr. Quicksolve to Harry Wake and Lulu Lyuer. "I think you're in big trouble, Harry," Officer Kautchya said.

"But I wasn't driving the boat this time! Lulu was driving. I was trying to stay out of trouble, so when I started drinking, I let her drive. She's usually a good driver. This was just an accident!" Harry insisted.

"Lulu," said Dr. Quicksolve, "tell us what happened."

"Just like Harry said, he asked me to drive. I was looking the other way, and I didn't see that other boat until it was too late. I stepped on the brakes as soon as I saw it, and I tried to swerve!" Lulu explained.

"You both can only get into more trouble if you don't admit to the obvious truth," Quicksolve said.

Why doesn't he believe their story?

Solution on page 93.

Burglars and Bludgeons

•••••••••

Dr. J. L. Quicksolve drove straight down the main road out of town for twenty miles before he got to the only turn he would make to get to Sara and Will Bludgeon's cabin north of the city. Beyond this was forty miles of wilderness. He drove a quarter mile through the dense woods before he reached the cabin. Three police officers were there waiting for him.

After greetings were exchanged, Officer Longshot explained, "Mrs. Bludgeon has been murdered. She was struck over the head with a blunt object, apparently by a burglar. Will Bludgeon, her husband, said he was upstairs in the shower when he heard his wife scream. He raced downstairs and found his wife lying dead in the family room. The burglar was gone."

"Did he call the police immediately, then?" asked Dr. Quicksolve.

"No, they don't have a telephone hooked up way out here in the woods. He was stopped by these officers for speeding just north of here. He said he was in a hurry to get help and to report the burglary and murder. They called us on their police radio," Officer Longshot said.

Dr. Quicksolve looked around the cabin and examined the broken back door. Finally, he turned to Officer Longshot and said, "Hold Will Bludgeon on suspicion of murdering his wife. There was no burglar."

Why does Dr. Quicksolve think Will Bludgeon killed his own wife?

Solution on page 93.

Eyewitness

•••••••

The small bank was in the middle of a small town, nestled between the hardware store on one side, the drugstore on the other, and a doctor's office beyond that. The bank had been robbed, and Police Chief Oz Baffled had called in Dr. J. L. Quicksolve for help.

"Dr. Quicksolve, we have witnesses, but a little confusion. The bank teller said a tall man in a long black coat and a ski mask came into the bank around nine o'clock this morning. There was no one else in the bank. The man looked around and drew a gun. He said it was a holdup and demanded money. The teller put two bags of money on the counter. Then the robber grabbed one of the bags and backed out of the bank."

"And the confusion you mentioned?" Dr. Quicksolve asked.

"Well, the teller said he then ran around the counter and out the door yelling. When he got outside there was a tall man half a block away with a coat on just like the robber's, but he wasn't running away. In fact, the tall man described the robber and gave us the license number of the getaway car, which he said barely slowed down as the man jumped in before it raced away. He said he had just come from the eye doctor two doors down, where he had a complete checkup for a new prescription. We checked, and the doctor's secretary said he's right about that. But the teller said he is pretty sure this witness was the bankrobber."

"I think you'd better arrest this man from the street right away," Dr. Quicksolve said.

Why does Dr. Quicksolve suspect the witness?

Solution on page 93.

Smith and Smith, Ex-Partners

•••••••••

There were two partners in the law firm of Smith and Smith. They were not brothers. One of them was dead. His body was found in his partner's house by his partner. Dr. J. L. Quicksolve was having lunch with his friend Sergeant Rebekah Shurshot discussing a case when she got the call on her portable receiver. They were at Mr. Smith's house in a matter of minutes, in spite of the traffic and rainy weather.

They hurried up to the door and were let in out of the rain by one of two officers who had gotten there just ahead of them. Mr. Smith was sitting at the kitchen table. The body of the other Mr. Smith lay covered nearby.

The back door that led to the backyard had obviously been jimmied with a knife. There was water on the floor, probably tracked in by the killer. Mr. Smith was explaining, "My partner, John, was here to meet me to talk over business. We had planned to meet here, and I left the front door unlocked in case he got here first. Apparently he did, and he was sitting here when someone broke in through the back door and stabbed him. I parked my car in the garage and came in through the side door there from the garage. The killer probably heard me coming and went out this back door when he heard me drive into the garage. I'm glad I didn't walk in on a killer with a knife!"

"Well," said Dr. Quicksolve, looking under the table.

Why was he looking under the table?

Solution on page 94.

Take Ten

●●●●●●●●

Junior, Dr. J. L. Quicksolve's son, was in the principal's office with his friend, Steve Swift, a younger boy whose ten-speed bike had been stolen from the bike rack behind school. Steve said he saw an older boy, Ted Theever, ride off on his bike. Ted was there too, telling his story.

"Steve saw me ride off in a hurry on my own ten-speed. It looks a lot like his. I wasn't stealing his bike. I was trying to help him get his bike back! I saw some kid who doesn't go to school here messing with Steve's bike. I said, 'Hey! That's not yours!' He jumped on the bike and rode off. I unlocked my bike and chased after him. He was way ahead, but I still almost caught him. I shifted into high to go up that steep hill on Maple, and I almost caught him there. Then he turned at the top of the hill. When I got to the top, he was out of sight. He must have turned into a driveway or gone behind a house there on Maple. I couldn't find him. I tried my best, but I just couldn't catch up with him."

"Is your bike new?" Junior asked Ted.

"No, I've had it for a couple years, but, like I said, it looks just like Steve's," Ted explained.

"I don't think your bike is like Steve's. I think it *is* Steve's!" Junior said.

Why is Junior so sure Ted stole the bike?

Solution on page 94.

Tracking Terrorists

•••••••••

Dr. J. L. Quicksolve never liked to follow a school bus for very long, at least not when it was frequently stopping for kids to get on or off. The school bus in front of him was not doing that, so he did not mind being behind it, although he was in a hurry. He was thinking about the call he had gotten from the police chief. He said there was to be a secret meeting between two small countries who had an ongoing border dispute for many years. There was hope of an agreement at this meeting. The problem was, there were terrorists from one side who had threatened to disrupt any such meeting.

The meeting was to be held at the Plaza Hotel, and the chief had asked Dr. Quicksolve for suggestions for protecting the visiting ambassadors. Dr. Quicksolve had given him several ideas and promised to be around and keep an eye out himself.

The school bus slowed briefly as it went over a set of railroad tracks, causing the need to downshift as it crossed over them. Dr. Quicksolve slowed before he reached the bumpy tracks and resumed his speed after he crossed them. The bus turned the next corner in the same direction Dr. Quicksolve was headed, so he was still stuck behind it.

Dr. Quicksolve reached for his carphone, pushed the number, and said, "This is J. L. Quicksolve. Tell the chief I think I have his terrorists in sight."

Why did Dr. Quicksolve say that?

Solution on page 94.

Murdered Miss

• • • • • • • •

The woman had been strangled. There were no witnesses and few clues. Her body was on the couch in the TV room. Two half-full glasses of lemonade were on the coffee table beside a half-empty bowl of popcorn. Dr. J. L. Quicksolve picked up each glass. The ice cubes clinked against the glass as he smelled each one for a scent of tobacco, lipstick, or anything that might be a clue. Nothing. He turned to the boyfriend who had called the police. "Tell me what you know," he said.

"Sharna and I had been sitting here watching TV, as you can see. I remembered I had some errands to run, so I left. When I came back I found her here like this. Then I called the police," he explained.

"How long were you gone?" asked Dr. Quicksolve.

"Oh, I was gone at least two hours. Hey! You don't suspect me, do you? I wouldn't have stayed here and called the police if I had done this. I tell you, I was gone for at least two hours! Anybody could have come in here, and she has an old boyfriend who was pretty jealous when she broke up with him. You'd better question him!"

"We will, certainly, but my guess is that he will have a much better alibi than you have," said Dr. Quicksolve.

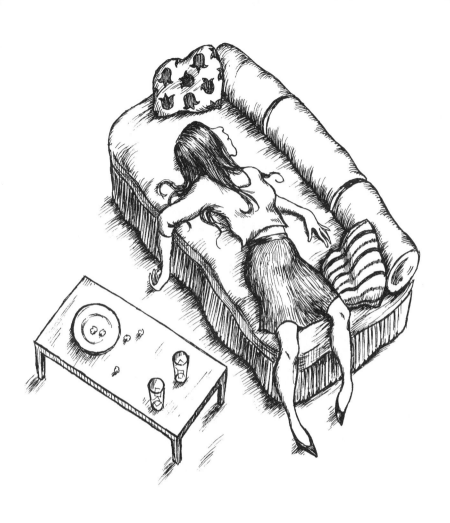

Why does Dr. Quicksolve suspect this boyfriend?

Solution on page 94.

Fishy Story

•••••••••

Dr. J. L. Quicksolve was better at catching criminals than he was at catching fish. He and his son, Junior, had been fishing from the riverbank for two hours. They had caught six fish. That is, Junior had caught six fish.

Dr. Quicksolve was distracted by a lot of commotion upriver a short distance. He had heard sirens. There were an ambulance and police cars. Seeing his father's distraction, and understanding, Junior said, "Sure, Dad, we can go see what happened."

Dr. Quicksolve recognized Deputy Paddlewater, a marine patrol officer with the Sheriff's Department. He was talking to another man. The man was soaking wet, clutching a blanket around himself. He was explaining about his friend's drowning.

"Dan and I are business associates and friends.

He hadn't ever canoed before, so I was steering us through the rapids. It got pretty rough. He must have fallen out sometime when we were going through the difficult parts. If he called out, I didn't hear him over the sound of the water. Anyway, I don't know when he fell out exactly. I didn't see him fall. When I got through the rough water I turned around, and he was just gone. I pulled over to this camp area, and I called the police."

Later Deputy Paddlewater told Dr. Quicksolve that the drowning victim had a suspicious bruise on the back of his head, as if he was hit with something, ". . . more like a paddle than a rock, the doctor said. There was no cut or abrasion, just the bruise and a bump."

Dr. Quicksolve said, "Well, with that and his story, you've got good reason to suspect foul play."

What was so wrong with the suspect's story?

Solution on page 94.

Dog Meet

• • • • • • • •

Junior, the son of the famous detective, Dr. J. L. Quicksolve, talked with his father. "Dad, I've got a problem," he said.

"Tell me what it is, son, and let's see what we can figure out."

"You know that track season starts pretty soon. I want to go out for track this year. I want to start running to get ready for it so I have a chance to make the team," Junior said.

"Great. So what's the problem?" Dr. Quicksolve asked.

"You know Tom, next door. He started running yesterday. He was chased by a dog, and he was almost bitten! His dad talked to the owner of that dog, and he said he would keep a better eye on him. But there are other dogs around. What can I do about them?"

"Well, you could carry a stick. That's a good idea

when you're out on those country roads by yourself. My other suggestion, and probably the best one, is to talk to the dog about it," Quicksolve told his son.

"Talk to the dog? What are you talking about? When a dog chases you, he isn't looking for conversation," Junior said.

"I don't know," Dr. Quicksolve told him, "but there is one word almost all dogs know. Use that word, and don't turn your back, and you'll probably be all right, unless it's a really vicious dog. That's where the club comes in. Most dogs are afraid of a man with a club."

"But what's the word?" Junior asked.

What is the word?

Solution on page 94.

Dit Dah Dilemma

• • • • • • • •

Dr. Quicksolve arrived at the scene just as the ambulance pulled away. "Thomas Graff," said Officer Longshot as Dr. Quicksolve approached. "He's unconscious. The medics say it looks like a coma. He may or may not recover, they said. He was struck by a bullet in the head sometime early this morning. He was found lying here in the parking lot in front of his office about an hour ago."

"Who found him?" Dr. Quicksolve asked.

"His partner, Sam Morris, found him lying here when he came in to work about seven o'clock this morning," Officer Longshot explained.

"Did Mr. Graff say anything to his partner or anyone before he became unconscious?"

"No, but he apparently tried to write a message here in the dirt. I guess he was too weak to tell what he was doing. It's just scratches, lines in the dirt."

Dr. Quicksolve looked at the marks etched in the ground. They were just lines—some short, some longer. There were three short lines, then a short and a longer line, followed by two longer lines—no legible words.

"Be sure Mr. Graff has an officer with him in the hospital, and bring Mr. Morris in for questioning," Dr. Quicksolve directed.

Why bring in Sam Morris?

Solution on page 94.

Jilted Joker

· · · · · · · · ·

"We're stumped," Officer Longshot said to Dr. J. L. Quicksolve. "This should be an open-and-shut case. We've got a suspect at the scene. We've got a motive. But we've got no weapon!"

"Tell me the whole story," Dr. Quicksolve said.

"A man was murdered at the circus. He was a trapeze artist. Our suspect is a clown who was jilted by one of the women who ride the elephants. Apparently, she jilted the clown for this trapeze guy. The clown was jealous and shot him behind one of the circus trucks," Officer Longshot explained.

"You said the clown was caught at the scene?" Dr. Quicksolve asked.

"Yes, he was seen selling balloons a few minutes before a shot was heard. A couple of people looked behind the wagon and found the clown standing next to the body. The guy was shot with a small-caliber pistol, probably a derringer, but we can't find it! The people who found him said the clown didn't have anything at all. We searched him at the scene—nothing. We got out the dogs to search for the weapon. We even looked up on top of the truck, but we just can't find the gun. There's no way, as far as I can see, that he could have gotten rid of the gun. We'll have to let him go."

"Maybe the gun was a little farther away than you could see, by the time you got there," Quicksolve said.

What did Dr. Quicksolve mean?

Answers on page 95.

Made in the Shades

•••••••••

"He was about six feet tall. He had brown hair, blue eyes, and a small scar on his left cheek." The clerk of the small country store was describing the man she said had robbed the store earlier that morning.

Standing there beside Dr. J. L. Quicksolve was Sergeant Rebekah Shurshot, who said, "Tell us exactly what happened, step-by-step."

"Well, this guy came in the door there. He went to that rack of sunglasses over there by the door, and he tried on several pairs while I waited on a couple of other customers, a lady buying a magazine and a boy buying candy. When no one else was in the store, he came over with a pair of the sunglasses on and asked me how they looked. I said they looked good. Then he said he would take them and a pack of cigarettes. When I turned my back to get the cigarettes, he pulled out a gun, and he said it was a stickup. He said to give him the money, so I did. Then he ran out and got into a blue car. I wasn't able to get the license, but he drove out the drive and then west. That's when I called the police," the clerk told them.

"There seems to be one flaw in this story," Dr. Quicksolve said.

What was wrong with the story?

Solution on page 95.

Bridge Play

It was a private farm road. A sign read "Private Road—Low Bridge—Keep Out." As Officer Long-arm drove under the bridge, he pointed up to it and explained to Dr. J. L. Quicksolve, "The suspects from an attempted robbery turned down this road. One of our cars chased them to that last corner, but he was forced off the road by the suspects in their truck. Everything happened too fast for him to get a license number. The backup police car got here about five minutes later. He stopped a minute to see that the first officer was all right. Then he went ahead. He passed under this bridge, passed another intersection, and went around the next curve where he found a truck like the first officer described. They were just packing up a portable air compressor. They said they had just had a flat tire."

"Do you believe the story about the flat?" Dr. Quicksolve asked.

"Well, they said they had one tire that was very low. There's no way to verify that. But the strange thing is that they claimed they weren't on the side road. They said they knew their truck was too high to get under the bridge. We measured, and they're right. It's one inch too high. They couldn't have driven under it, so we let them go."

"Get them back," is all Dr. Quicksolve said.

PRIVATE ROAD
LOW BRIDGE
KEEP OUT!

Why?

Solution on page 95.

ANSWERS

Brotherly Love (page 6)—Pat knew Tom's body was found at the cottage when no one told him.

Station Stickup (page 8)—The attendant claims the robbers drove in and pumped their gas after five, but the pumps are shut off and require prepayment.

Backyard Bandit (page 10)—Mr. Dare claims he could hear someone picking a lock above the noise of a lawnmower, and that he saw a man through an eight-foot hedge well enough to describe him.

The Doubtable Burglary (page 12)—A burglar couldn't have used Mr. Doubtable's screwdriver because it was kept in the basement of the locked house with the other tools. The window had to be jimmied by someone who already had been in the house to get the screwdriver.

Locker Caper (page 14)—Jason knew the videotapes were missing even though no one had mentioned them.

Cross-Eyed Witness (page 16)—Looking out the front window, Mr. Menace could not have seen anyone break down the back door.

Flying Thief (page 18)—She said the alarm didn't work because the electricity was off, yet the security camera was working.

Reflection of a Crime (page 20)—The reflection, like a mirror, would make the scar appear to be on the opposite side of the face.

A Puzzling Story (page 22)—She must have found that last puzzle piece after Mrs. Charmsworth and Leroy had left. He was ready early and left right from the unfinished puzzle. She must have found the missing piece when she came back with the burglars.

Inside Job (page 24)—The butler must be lying. He claimed he could see such details as a thin red moustache and a scar on a man clear out by the street in the dark.

Welcome Bandit (page 26)—Germain apparently let this robber in even though he was wearing a mask and could be seen through the glass door. He must be lying.

Holey Donuts (page 28)—He claims he opened the safe after he was tied up and blindfolded.

Breakfast Break-In (page 30)—She said she put the teakettle on even before she saw the burglar. Then she went upstairs, came down and saw the safe was open, and went back upstairs to call and wait for Dr. Quicksolve. In all that time the water had not begun to boil. If it was turned up hot enough to boil, it could not have taken that long to begin to whistle.

Rose's Robbery (page 32)—She claims she was locked in her car. That can't be done. You can always open a car door from the inside.

Skating Rink Robbery (page 34)—Frank said he heard a noise from the soundproof office while he was in the main room with the loud music.

Ransom Rescue (page 36)—John wanted a lineup because he knew the girl was blindfolded and wouldn't recognize him. Frank couldn't fool a lie-detector test.

Barefoot Liar (page 38)—How did Mr. Crookby, in bare feet and just out of bed, use a phone surrounded by broken glass? He probably had shoes on and went outside to break the window to make it look like a robbery. He made the call and then took his shoes off to make it look as if he had just come from bed.

Pennyroll's Money Bags (page 40)—Heading back toward the bank, they should not have reached the money bag before they reached the corner where Mr. Pennyroll jumped out of the car. He must have made up the story about kidnappers.

Jacked Up (page 42)—They didn't get the wheels, but they left the car jacked up with the jack from their trunk.

Now You See It (page 44)—Frank Lee got back an hour later than usual, yet the cook had timed dinner just right for his return. He would have known how late Mr. Lee would be, because he was the one who took gas out of the motorcycle to give himself time to steal the paintings.

McMugger (page 46)—You get a bag from a fast food restaurant when you get your food to go and a tray when you stay and eat there. He is lying.

Dark Shadows (page 49)—Mr. Grimsox has claimed to see shadows of men walking too close to the side of the house to see them on a rainy evening. Even if there were shadows, he would not be able to see them against the house from upstairs. The dark house would have prevented light from casting shadows the other way.

Crooked Interview (page 52)—Carl said he had never been to prison, yet he knew the old slang for a prison guard, a "screw."

Cool Mickey (page 54)—Mickey could have frozen the poison into the center of the ice cubes. That way he knew the drink would be safe for a few minutes until the ice began to melt. He figured that drinking from her glass and then leaving would give him a great alibi.

Missing Money (page 57)—Dr. Quicksolve suspects the two salesmen are ringing doorbells and if no one is home, slipping in quickly, taking what they can hide in their pockets or coats, and getting out fast. Purses make good targets because they are often left by the door. He hopes to catch them entering or leaving his house.

Motorcycle Mischief (page 59)—Tom said he put his right leg down when he stopped, hence the bandage. Motorcycle safety classes teach you to put your left foot down first, because the brake is on the right side!

Bop-n-Rob (page 62)—Mr. Drumhead was hit from behind on the left side of his head, so the robber was very probably left-handed. Making a "mirror image" as they wrote tells us one of the men is the left-handed robber, and the other one is an innocent right-hander.

Boat Bash (page 64)—Small speedboats are run and stopped with a throttle: There is no footbrake to step on. Lulu has probably never driven one.

Burglars and Bludgeons (page 66)—Mr. Bludgeon was caught for speeding north of the cabin, apparently running away from town and the telephones into the wilderness.

Eyewitness (page 68)—Coming straight from the eye doctor, he would have had drops in his eyes that would make it nearly impossible to see the license number of a passing car. The eye drops also explain why the robber took only one bag. He couldn't see clearly!

Smith and Smith, Ex-Partners (page 70)—He wanted to see if Mr. Smith's shoes were wet. If they were, he must have sneaked in the back door to surprise his partner and kill him, and Dr. Quicksolve would have solved another case, because, coming through the garage, they would be dry.

They were. He had. He did.

Take Ten (page 72)—Ted said he has had a ten-speed bike for two years, yet he doesn't know that you switch to a lower gear to climb steep hills!

Tracking Terrorists (page 74)—Dr. Quicksolve suspected the school bus might contain the terrorists because a school bus is required to come to a full stop at a railroad crossing. Drivers are also taught to not shift as they go over the tracks.

Murdered Miss (page 76)—He claims to have been gone for over two hours before he even called the police, yet the ice in the glasses had not melted.

Fishy Story (page 78)—He said he was steering because Dan did not know how. Then he said Dan fell out, and he did not know it until he turned around. If he were steering, he would have been in the back of the canoe. He probably hit Dan from behind and saw him fall.

Dog Meet (page 80)—It's what people use when they want their pets (or children) to stop doing something. The word is "no!"

Dit Dah Dilemma (page 82)—The lines in the dirt are the Morse Code pattern for S-A-M. Apparently, Mr. Graff was trying to tell who shot him without being too obvious to the killer, who may have seen what he did.

Jilted Joker (page 84)—Minutes before, the clown had a bunch of helium-filled balloons. He did not have them when he was discovered. He must have let them go—after he tied the derringer to them. The evidence flew away!

Made in the Shades (page 86)—She described the man as having blue eyes, yet he only approached her after he put sunglasses on. She could not have seen the color of his eyes!

Bridge Play (page 88)—Dr. Quicksolve knows that if they had a portable air compressor, they could have let enough air out of all their tires to lower their truck enough to get under the bridge. Then they could refill their tires quickly, pretending to be fixing one tire.

Index

Answer pages are in italics